Big Machines

Big Machines Build!

Catherine Veitch

Heinemann
LIBRARY
Chicago, Illinois

Edited by Helen Cox Cannons and Kathryn Clay
Designed by Tim Bond and Peggie Carley
Picture research by Mica Brancic and Tracy Cummins
Production by Helen McCreath
Originated by Capstone Global Library Ltd
Printed and bound in China by Leo Paper Group

18 17 16 15 14
10 9 8 7 6 5 4 3 2 1

Cataloging-in-publication information is on file
with the Library of Congress.
ISBN 978-1-4846-0584-4 (Hardcover)
ISBN 978-1-4846-0591-2 (eBook PDF)

Photo Credits

Alamy: © Clynt Garnham Industry, 18, 19, 22d, © imagebroker/Tom Mueller, 14,
© RJH_COMMON, 16, 17, 22b; Corbis: © Construction Photography, 21; Komatsu:
10, 11, 22a; Liebherr: 8, 9, 12, 13, 22c; Shutterstock: Dmitry Kalinovsky, 4, 5,
Jarous, 6, 7, back cover, Kletr, 15, Krivosheev Vitaly, 20, back cover, SteveWoods,
front cover; SuperStock: Science and Society, 4

Every effort has been made to contact copyright holders of material reproduced
in this book. Any omissions will be rectified in subsequent printings if notice is
given to the publisher.

All the Internet addresses (URLs) given in this book were valid at the time of go-
ing to press. However, due to the dynamic nature of the Internet, some
addresses may have changed, or sites may have changed or ceased to exist
since publication. While the author and publisher regret any inconvenience this
may cause readers, no responsibility for any such changes can be accepted by
either the author or the publisher.

Contents

Some words are shown in bold, **like this.** You can find out what they mean by looking in the glossary.

Road Roller

Heavy road rollers are used to repair roads and paths. They flatten hot tar to make the ground **level**.

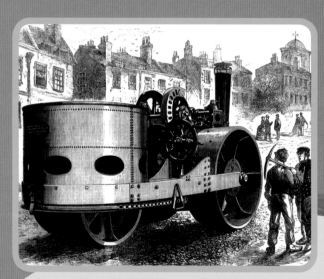

Road rollers are sometimes called steamrollers. This steamroller was built by Thomas Aveling more than 150 years ago.

Super
Big
Mighty
Size

roller

tar

5

Punch Power

This machine is a huge hammer called a hydraulic hammer. It breaks up rocks and **concrete**.

Super
Big Mighty
Size

Hydraulic hammers are also called breakers or hoe rams.

Heavy Truck

Meet one of the world's largest dump trucks. It is used to carry soil on mining sites.

This truck can haul 406 tons (368 metric tons). That's the same as carrying 66 adult elephants!

Super

Big   Mighty

Size

Big Bulldozer

A bulldozer's huge **blade** shoves away massive amounts of **rubble**, rock, and soil.

The biggest bulldozer in the world is as large as a house!

blade

Big Super Size Mighty

Flying High

The world's tallest crane is 814 feet (248 meters) tall. It's the length of about 50 giraffes standing on top of each other!

Super
Big Mighty
Size

This crane can lift about 661 tons (600 metric tons). That's as many as 350 cars at once!

Super Scoop

The world's largest shovel can carry 94 tons (85 metric tons). That's the same as lifting about 50 cars at once!

Super
Big Mighty
Size

groove

The **grooves** on these thick tires help to grip bumpy ground.

Crazy Crusher

This huge machine is called a crusher. It is used to break up large rocks into **gravel**.

Deep Digger

Check out this giant digging machine, or **excavator**. Its 20 buckets scoop up coal. The buckets are so big that one accidentally picked up a bulldozer once!

The digger is so heavy that when it is driven over roads, the roads are destroyed.

Super

Big

Mighty

Size

buckets

Sizing Things Up

Weight	up to 13 tons (12 metric tons)
Height.	up to 10 feet (3 meters)
Drum length	up to 6.6 feet (2 meters)
Tire width.	up to 8.9 feet (2.7 meters)
Engine.	137 horsepower

drum

Weight	up to 29 tons (26 metric tons)
Height	up to 14.5 feet (4.4 meters)
Blade weight	up to 8 tons (7.3 metric tons)
Track length	13 feet (4 meters)
Engine	up to 266 horsepower

Bulldozer

blade

Quiz

How much of a Machine Mega-Brain are you?
Can you match each machine name to its correct photo?

excavator • crusher
bulldozer • crane

1

2

3

4

Check the answers on the opposite page
to see if you got all four correct.

Glossary

blade the cutting part of a machine that has a thin, sharp edge

concrete a mixture of cement, water, sand, and gravel that hardens when dry

excavator a machine that is used for digging

gravel a mixture of sand, pebbles, and broken rocks

groove a long, narrow channel cut into a surface

level to make something flat

rubble the broken pieces that are left when a building falls down

Quiz Answers:
1. bulldozer 2. crusher 3. crane 4. excavator

Find Out More

Books

Gilbert, Sara. *Dump Trucks*. Machines that Build. Mankato, Minn.: Creative Education, 2009.

Sutton, Sally. *Demolition*. Somerville, Mass.: Candlewick, 2012.

Websites

www.capstonekids.com/explore/Mighty-Machines/index.html
www.cat.com/equipment

Index